THE
DESERT DRIVER'S
MANUAL

Jim Stabler

CONTENTS

INTRODUCTION

This book outlines all the factors that need to be considered if you intend to drive in the desert. It has been produced in a size convenient for carrying with you in the glove box of your vehicle and for use as reference. It has been based on experience in the Middle East, but is applicable to any of the world's desert areas.

The sections on planning, desert driving and recovery techniques are detailed and I hope will give the reader the basic knowledge essential for enjoyable and safe treks through the desert.

The sections on vehicle problems, navigation and survival cannot be comprehensive in so small a book, but they attempt to outline the main points that you should know before attempting your own expeditions. The book makes no attempt to replace proper and qualified instruction in these important skills.

I am indebted to Dr John G Gibbons, another great desert enthusiast, who contributed to the basic notes on first aid. He stresses that if you intend to travel regularly in the desert you would be wise to undertake a first aid training course.

I also wish to thank Harry Jones with whom I have spent many pleasurable hours in the desert driving, digging and perfecting the techniques described in this book. Thanks also to Andy Spencer for his invaluable help on the vehicle problems section.

It also should be stressed that your first treks should always be in the company of experienced desert travellers. With the knowledge gleaned from this book and practise in the company of others you will soon perfect your skills. But always expect the unexpected and be prepared.

Desert driving brings tremendous rewards in the sights that you will see, and in the comradeship and the personal challenge. I used to wonder what men like Doughty, Thesiger and Lawrence saw in the desert but after my own travels throughout the deserts of the Middle East, I too have been bitten by the bug and find the peace and beauty of the land both inspiring and awesome.

Finally, please remember that desert driving is potentially a dangerous pursuit and people die every year trying to cross the world's deserts. This book gives you the basic requirements and rules to undertake it safely but the author can in no way be held liable for anything that happens as a result of your travels.

J.S.

3

THE RULES

These are the fundamental rules for all desert driving and are ignored at your peril:

1. YOU MUST HAVE A FOUR-WHEEL DRIVE VEHICLE.

2. NEVER ATTEMPT DESERT TRAVEL OR OFF-ROAD DRIVING WITH FEWER THAN THREE VEHICLES
   FOUR ARE IDEAL
   MORE THAN FIVE AND YOU START TO LOSE THEM.

3. EVEN ON DAY TRIPS TELL SOMEONE WHERE YOU ARE GOING AND STICK TO YOUR PLAN.

4. PREPARE FOR A DAY TRIP AS THOROUGHLY AS FOR A MAJOR EXPEDITION.

5. IF YOUR VEHICLES BREAK DOWN OR GET STUCK **STAY WITH THEM**.

THESE SIMPLE RULES COULD SAVE YOUR LIFE

PLANNING

Please remember that even day trips need planning. You can get stuck just as badly 30 km down a local wadi as in the middle of the Nefud.

Advice
The advice of people who have been to your intended destination before is invaluable and can be more reliable than maps or guides. Moreover, some sand is forever shifting. Ask friends to draw maps, say what the going was like, how far they got in what time, and where the petrol stops were.

Maps
Available maps tend to be large scale and out of date. They are, however, better than nothing and should always be carried.

The sketch maps which abound in the Middle East should be treated with care as what is accurate in one person's mind may not be very accurate on the ground.

The best advice when driving in a new area is to keep a record of where you go. A list of bearings and distances from easily recognisable landmarks will allow you to retrace your steps if all else fails. It's also worthwhile looking back once in a while so you will know how the terrain looks in case you do have to turn back.

Distances
You also have to be very careful about estimating the distances that you expect to travel in a day. On roads it can easily be 500 km; on good tracks say 300 km; on rocky surfaces or sand it might only be possible to do 100 km. When the conditions are really bad you may be lucky to do 50 km. Plan accordingly and use these figures as a guideline:
- 6 hours driving per day (this allows for stops in an 8 hour travelling day) in a 4-wheel drive Landrover.
- When planning desert driving, the following should be your guidelines (without a getting lost allowance):
  - ◆ Over good known tracks   200 km maximum
  - ◆ Along wadis and over rougher surfaces 100 km maximum
  - ◆ Over sand dunes   50 km maximum

Petrol Consumption
Your petrol consumption is difficult to estimate as it depends on your type of car, terrain, temperature and heaviness of your pedal foot. The following figures hold good for Landrover 110s and most other large engined vehicles:

Surface	Ave. Speed		Petrol Consumption			Notes
	MPH	KPH	MPG	KPG	KP10L*	
Tarmac	60	100	15	24	50	1
Good tracks	30	50	10	16	35	1
Hard wadi sand	20	30	8	12	26	2
Rough/rocky terrain	15	24	8	12	26	1
Soft sand	10	16	5	8	18	3

Notes
1. Using high gearbox and 2-wheel drive
2. Using high gearbox and 4-wheel drive
3. Using low gearbox and 4-wheel drive

* KP10L is the distance travelled in km for every 10 litres of fuel.

On rough, trackless surfaces and especially sand dunes you may have to travel over twice the straight line distances. Calculate MPG accordingly. For diesel engined vehicles you can normally double the above.

Time of year
Remember in your planning that the time of year will affect your journey plans. In winter, the conditions are cooler but the days are slightly shorter. In summer, travel is far more arduous and the water requirements, clothing and camping equipment will differ considerably from an extremely cold winter trip. You also need to be careful in the spring when heavy rains and flash flooding occur – surprisingly, perhaps, the most dangerous hazards in the desert.

Equipment
The following three sections list the equipment you will need to carry, but first a word of caution on the stowage of all the equipment:
● Ensure everything is securely lashed down and cannot move. Nothing is more disconcerting than your sand ladders whizzing past your right ear and through the windscreen when you do your first real emergency stop.
● Ensure that the items you need to use first or in an emergency are easily accessible. Nothing is gained by your first aid kit, sand ladders, shovel or tow-rope being stored underneath everything else.
    You may wish to stow certain rescue and recovery items on the outside of the vehicle but beware: roof racks are not built to be loaded with the kitchen sink! There is a roof rack weight limit, normally about 50 kg; respect this. We once had a vehicle in the party with a very heavily loaded roof rack that went airborne over a

rise in the ground and landed heavily. When the driver stopped and tried to get out of the vehicle he couldn't, all the doors had been jammed shut by a roof that was now about an inch lower. Also, the more weight you store on top the more easily you will roll over.

Party composition

Ideally, the party should consist of five vehicles. This allows you to commit two vehicles to a recovery and, if all else fails, you still have two vehicles to drive out in. Fewer than this means you can only commit one vehicle to the recovery, which is not always enough. Any more than five makes it very difficult to control the party and ensure everyone sticks together, so it is worth considering splitting them into two groups. Within the party you should ideally have the following specialists:

- The party leader (normally in charge of navigation).
- At least one more navigator to check leader's calculations and directions.
- A first-aider.
- A vehicle mechanic.
- Someone who speaks the local language.
- An admininstrator to organise meals, packing lists, etc.

It is essential to plan the trip and discuss what everyone will be expected to take and who is responsible for each aspect of the plan. This can cut down on the number of items carried by each vehicle (and the number of items forgotten). To help, you will find a format for a planning document on page 63. It is not exhaustive, but will give you a basis on which to build.

Telling people where you are going

It is essential that you complete some form of proforma, noting who is in the party, where you are going, when you're setting off, when you're expected back, what communications you have and, finally, what is the deadline for calling out the emergency services. Give this to a reliable friend asking him to call out the emergency services if you're not back by your deadline. Make sure you contact him on your return.

A example of a suitable proforma is shown on page 62.

Finally, ensure you plan your drive and drive your plan. This way, the rescue services will know where to look.

VEHICLE PREPARATION AND CHECKS

Checks

The following **must** all be checked before you attempt desert driving – it may be boring but the one thing you don't check will be missing when you need it badly:

- Tyres, their condition and pressure (including the spares).
- Engine oil level, and see if there are any leaks.
- Radiator water level (and have you got a spare can for the vehicle?).
- Petrol (and have you got spare cans as required?).
- Fan belts – are they tight and in good condition?
- Battery – is it topped up and firmly secured?
- Is the windscreen washer bottle full (no soap – you may want to drink it).
- Lights – are they all working?
- Security of roof rack, equipment and accessories.
- Have you got all the documents you need?
- Have you got all the equipment you need? (If camping, make sure you've got the tent poles and pegs.)
- Have you got all the extras you may need (see the attached lists)?
- Horn (one of the most important items on your car).

Note: On long trips these vehicle checks should be carried out every morning.

Vehicle equipment lists

The following lists of spares and equipment that you need to carry may seem long and complicated but, believe me, they have been refined over many years by experienced desert travellers. They are also a minimum requirement. Many people carry much more, including major spares packs for their vehicles. There are many excellent sources for equipment and spare packs, including – most likely – your local 4-wheel drive dealers who will offer you advice on what extras to take. Some will also offer you spares packs for longer expeditions on a sale or return basis.

Vehicle tools, spares and recovery items

Workshop manual	Vehicle handbook	12V Tester
Paintbrush (dusting)	HT lead set	Spare bulbs
Spark plugs	Insulating tape	Jump leads
Duct (GP) tape	Cloth (rags)	Hose (jubilee) clips
Drive belts (3)	Adjustable spanner	Spares fuses
Screwdrivers	Length iron wire	Spanners
Length electric wire	Hammer	Tyre levers (3)
Metric spanners	Tyre pressure gauge	Mole wrench
Tubeless tyre repair kit	Pliers	Inner tube repair kit

Spark plug spanner	Spare inner tubes	Hacksaw
Foot pump	Electric air pump	Gloves
Wheel chocks	Torch	Funnel for petrol cans
Siphon tube	Araldite	Gasket compound
Brake fluid	Hydraulic jack	Radiator sealant
Engine oil	Distilled water	Hand cleaner
Points, condenser, rotor & cap	Wheel brace	Socket Set

Recovery equipment
- Sand ladders.
- Shovel.
- Base boards (for using jack on soft ground).
- Heavy duty 25 m tow-rope.
- Short 8 m tow-rope.
- Rope or tape strops.
- Shackles x 6.
- Snatch block.*
- KERR snatch tow-rope.*
- Portable winch (if owned).*
- Air bag jack.*
- High lift jack.*

Safety equipment
- Spare car keys (NB: tie the car keys to the steering column so you can't lose them by dropping them in the sand).
- Sunshade for windscreen: the plastic bubble shades are best as they double as excellent radiator covers when you're going through water.
- Fire extinguishers.
- Large plastic or canvas sheet, complete with bungees and poles to use as a sunshade.*
- Small canvas sheet to put on the ground when you work on the vehicle (a nut dropped in the sand is never found!).*
- Fluorescent orange warning panels to use as markers.*
- A couple of bamboo poles and flags. If you stick them at a high point in the sand you can see them for miles and know where you came from.*
- A 2m x 2m clear plastic sheet to use as a solar still (see page 52).*
- A flashing light or small strobe light to be used as an emergency beacon at night.*
- Search and rescue radio beacon (SARBE), if legal and available.*
- Two way radios, if legal and available.*
- Mobile telephone if available.*

* These items can be considered to be group equipment and only one set carried. Larger groups should carry two sets or more.

PERSONAL EQUIPMENT AND PREPARATION

Water
The most important supply. Remember, when it's really hot you'll be drinking about 10 litres a day; so you need 20 litres per person per day to allow for cooking and washing. A good way of carrying water for drinking is to take a bottle of water, empty out about a glass full and then freeze the bottle. This allows the ice to expand without bursting the bottle. In a coolbox, ice melts slowly, providing cold water even on the hottest day.

Food
Ensure you take sufficient food and of the kind that will not spoil in the heat. Chocolate, for example, isn't much good when the temperature is 45°C. Make the best use of cool boxes and frozen items to keep the food at its best. Also wrap in plastic bags all items that may get water-logged. You can then fill the spaces in the cool box with ice cubes.

Clothing
Loose cotton clothing should be worn in summer, but remember to take extras for the winter when it can be very cold at night. Always have long sleeves, trousers and hats available in case you have to work in the sun or if the insects get hungry. Strong, sensible footwear is also a necessity: sandals may be cooler but you can't walk or work in them. In summer, gloves are essential to handle bare metal that gets too hot to touch.

Money and documents
Remember to carry some money, including change for the telephone, and all the documents you could possibly require, such as the following:
- Driving licence.
- Identity cards/passports/*Iqamas* (residence permit, in Arab countries).
- Letters of authority to travel.
- Vehicle documents.
- Insurance details.
- Letter of permission to use a company vehicle.
- Letter of authority to visit sites of interest.
- List of useful telephone numbers so that you can call for help.

Extras
Camera	Sunglasses
Spare film	Bags and boxes to put everything in
Binoculars	Straps to tie everything down
Personal medicines	Toilet rolls
Short wave radio	Insect repellent
Matches/lighter	

CAMPING EQUIPMENT

The following is a list of some of the camping equipment that you may wish to take and again tends to be the minimum requirement. Some do it in style and carry everything including generators, lights and even a microwave oven. But remember, you have to store it somewhere in the vehicle and the heavier the vehicle, the more easily it will become stuck and the more difficult it will be to recover:

- Tent with sown-in groundsheet, extra long steel pegs and a hammer.
- Table and chairs.
- Cooker.
- Spare gas and a lighter.
- Cooking and eating utensils.
- Washing-up bowl.
- Sleeping bags.
- Camp beds.
- Lights.
- Extra torches.

You should also be careful when choosing a campsite. I find the best to be flat sandy areas sheltered from the worst winds. I always avoid the following:

- Very rocky sites where you will have difficulty putting up the tent.
- Sites close to water – the insects will have you for tea.
- Sites too close to villages, animals, animal droppings or rubbish – all of which attract insects too.
- Wadis or dry river beds: rain, even miles away, could cause a flash flood. In the Middle East, people die every year in flash floods.

NAVIGATION

Outline

Again, it is beyond the scope of this book to be a full treatise on map-reading and navigation. I will only mention the main elements you must know before venturing into the desert. There are many excellent and detailed books on map-reading and navigation and you would do well to buy, read and master one. This is a key skill, so don't rely on the leader of the party to do all the navigation. Do your own measuring and estimating and check regularly with the others in the group to ensure you all know where you are. If the leader is suddenly taken ill or you are separated from the rest of your group it is essential you know where you are, where you've come from and where you're going.

Finally, even if you have your car fitted with the most modern GPS and electronic compasses, remember both can, and at the most inconvenient time will, fail. Make sure you know how to use your map and compass and make a written record of where you've been.

Map reading

The key elements of map-reading that you must master are as follows:
- Magnetic and Grid North.
- Maps and scales.
- Grid references and latitude/longitude.
- Using a compass.
- Bearings.
- Finding your position by resection.

The Norths

- Grid North. This is the line that runs vertically up and down your map, indicated by the grid lines drawn on the map.
- Magnetic North. This is the line connecting your position to the Magnetic North Pole and the direction in which your compass needle points.

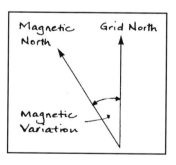

The position of the Magnetic North Pole varies each year and the difference between this and the Grid North is called the *magnetic variation*. You must correct your magnetic bearings by this amount to convert them to bearings on the map. Most maps have both Norths indicated on them. Beware – not all maps are drawn with North at the top of them! This is often true with maps produced locally in the Middle East where the top of the map points towards the holy city of Makkah.

The value of magnetic variation, sometimes called magnetic declination, is normally found at the bottom of maps along with the key.

Maps and scales

Maps are drawn to different scales which are indicated by a ratio such as 1:250,000. This indicates the number that you have to multiply a length on the map by in order to obtain the distance over the ground. For example with a 1:250,000 map, 1 cm on the map equates to 250,000

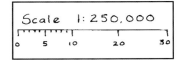

cm on the ground, i.e. 2.5 km. Most maps also show the scale as a small ruler visually depicting the equivalent ground measurement.

For full details on what symbols mean refer to the key on the map.

Grid references

Most maps are divided into regular squares by grid lines drawn on the map. These are numbered at 1 km spacings. Reference to a point is often made by quoting the grid reference. You should note that the grid references drawn on most small scale maps, i.e. 1:50,000 and 1:25,000, are based on the local grid systems in use in their country of origin. Grid references are normally used:

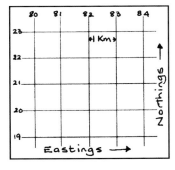

- in a country with efficient mapping.
- working over relatively short distances.

You can work out a grid reference by the following method of estimation:

- Go easterly along the vertical grid lines (the Eastings) and note the two figures on the last Easting before the point. i.e. 42.
- Estimate the distance in tenths of a grid square to the next grid line, i.e. 5.
- These 3 figures give you the first half of the grid reference, i.e. 425.
- Repeat the procedure going North along the other grid lines (the Northings).
- This gives you the second half of the grid reference, i.e. 363.
- Put both together, Eastings first and Northings second, for the full grid reference, i.e. 425363.

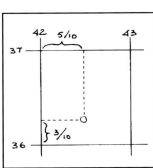

You should note that because of this numbering scheme, similar grid references will recur every 100 km. You therefore need to precede this grid reference with the number or letters that designate your particular 100 km square in order to create the final, unique, reference within that grid system.

Latitude and longitude

The use of latitude and longitude obviate the problems of recurring grid references and local grid systems (all of which arise from the problem of trying to represent the curved surface of a sphere on a flat piece of paper – the map). They are imaginary lines drawn on the earth's surface:

Latitude. The horizontal lines are called lines of latitude and are equally divided (on a sphere) into 90 degrees in either direction. The equator is 0 degrees, the North Pole 90 degrees North and the South Pole 90 degrees South.

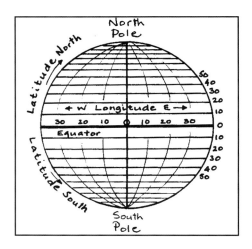

Longitude. The vertical lines are lines of longitude. 0 degrees longitude passes through Greenwich and the rest of the world divided into 180 degrees to the West and East. The 180 degree line, where the two directions of measuring meet again on the opposite side of the world to Greenwich, is called the International Date Line.

Note : The lines of longitude converge as they approach the two Poles.

References are calculated in a similar method to that of grid references. First you measure the latitude in terms of degrees minutes and seconds (or decimal minutes). After this is then added the direction of measurement from the equator north or south.

The longitude is measured similarly but the direction of measurement from Greenwich added, i.e. Riyadh in Saudi Arabia is approximately 24 degrees 45 minutes North 46 degrees 40 minutes East (or 24°45' N 46°40' E)

These references are the ones normally used with modern navigational systems such as GPS (Global Positioning System) which uses small handheld or vehicle mounted satellite receivers to calculate your position. Again there are variations upon this system stemming from locally used datum points. Look at the map to see what system is in use. Normally this will be WGS 84, but there are local variations.

USING A COMPASS

A handheld compass

Most modern hand held compasses combine both a compass and a protractor to enable you accurately and simply to plot bearings directly onto a map. The diagram illustrates the various parts. Most compasses come with excellent instruction booklets: you should study yours carefully as some even have a built-in offset to allow for magnetic variation.

Remember: however unlikely you think the reading from your compass is, TRUST IT.

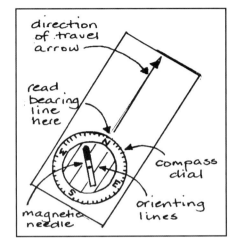

Setting the map

First, you must use the compass to set the map. This means aligning the map with the ground so that directions on the ground equate to directions on the map. Thus you will be able to identify ground features more easily. Place the compass on the map and set the orienting lines to due North parallel to the grid lines on the map. The magnetic variation need not be taken into account unless it is very large. Next rotate the map and compass until the compass needle is pointing to the North marker on the dial. Your map is now aligned with the ground and directions on the map equate to direction on the ground.

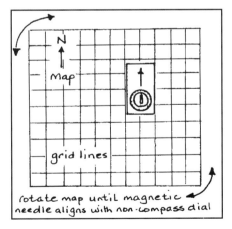

Bearings

This operation uses the compass purely as a protractor and the compass needle plays no part. That is why it has been omitted from the diagram.

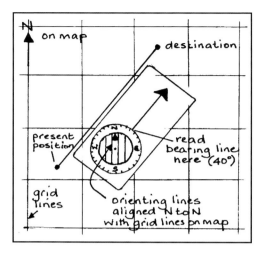

If you know where you are and where you want to go on the map, how do you use your compass to find the direction over the ground that you need to travel?

First you need to work out the grid bearing from the map.

Work out your position on the map and the point to which you wish to go. If it makes it easier for you, draw a line joining both.

Set the compass with the direction of travel lines (use the edge of the base for simplicity) on the line you have drawn and pointing towards the destination.

Now align the orienting lines on the compass dial with the North grid lines on the map so that the North arrow on the dial (not the magnetic needle) is pointing to the north end of the map grid lines.

Read the bearing from where the direction of travel arrow meets the compass dial. This is the grid bearing, i.e 40°.

In order to convert this to a magnetic bearing, we must now allow for magnetic variation. You add the variation to the bearing (conversely if you have taken a magnetic bearing you must subtract the variation). I use an old mnemonic: Grid to Mag add – Mag to Grid get rid.

Note: This is true where the magnetic variation is to the West of Grid North. If in your area of the world the Magnetic North is to the East of the Grid North then reverse the calculation. Where the variation is only one or two degrees, I ignore it completely since most bearings are not accurate to that degree anyway.

So, if the variation is 8° this would give a magnetic bearing of 48°.

The next stage is to set this on the compass and use the magnetic needle to show you the direction over the ground.

Move the compass dial around so that the direction of travel arrow moves from the 40° calculated earlier to the magnetic bearing of 48°.

Hold the compass horizontally and gradually turn it until the magnetic needle and the orienting arrow align north to north.

Now look along the direction of travel lines. This is the direction to the destination.

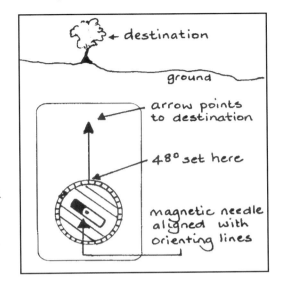

The reverse procedure can also be undertaken where you take a magnetic bearing using your compass and convert this to a line on the map. This is explained more fully in the next section.

Finding Your Position on the Map

First, set the map as explained earlier. If you can see prominent ground features which you can recognise on the map then you can use these to plot your position on the map as follows:

Point the direction of travel arrow as accurately as possible to the known ground feature.

Carefully rotate the compass housing until the magnetic needle and the orienting lines are aligned north to north.

Check you are still pointed towards the feature and adjust the housing as required.

Note: Some compasses have a hinged lid with a mirror that make this much easier.

The reading on the dial is then your magnetic bearing to the feature. Again use the rule for magnetic variation correction – subtract the variation.

Set the grid bearing on the compass which you will now use again as a protractor.

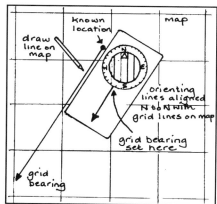

Start at the known feature and rotate the compass until the orienting lines align north to north with the grid lines. Make sure the direction of travel line, or, as shown, the edge of the base, starts at the map position of the feature. Mark the bearing on the map.

If you now repeat this with another known feature, ideally at 90° to the first, you can then draw a second line on the map. Where they cross is your approximate position.

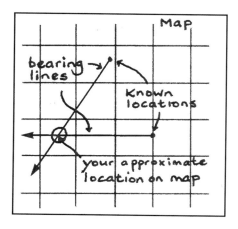

SKETCH MAPS

All the above operations with maps and compasses work well if you have accurate maps. But what if you're going into an area with poor maps, only large scale maps or even no maps at all? In these circumstances the only way to explore the country is to draw sketch maps of where you go. This is the method by which I drew all my early maps of the deserts around Riyadh in the 1980s. These should be based on distance driven and bearings to major features. When you do this, always remember to look behind you and sketch that too. After all, that will be the way you're facing on the drive back.

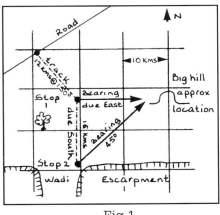

Fig 1

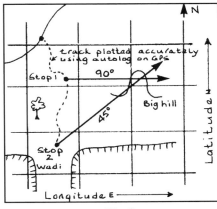

Fig 2

Use squared paper with a scale drawn on it. Carefully log each leg of your journey, marking any important features or key crossing points. If you follow this procedure, logging each leg with distance and bearing to easily recognised features, you will always be able to find your way back. (Fig 1)

One very useful procedure to prevent disorientation when you are exploring sand dunes is to place flags (bamboo poles with rags tied to the top) on the high points as you go through the dunes. This way you will be able to check your approximate position and have aiming marks if you are forced to drive back.

Note: This procedure is made much easier if you have a GPS. You can start with a sheet of paper with the latitude and longitude lines drawn on it at a known scale. You can then mark your route accurately and note the approximate locations of key features. (Fig 2)

Use of the sun

When driving along unknown tracks, I rarely rely on vehicle compasses but tend to use the position of the sun's shadows on the vehicle as a guide that I am travelling in the correct direction. I use a handheld compass to note a feature in the direction I need to travel and then point the vehicle in that direction, at the same time noting the position of the sun's shadows on the vehicle. If the shadows move greatly (allowing for the normal twisting and turning of tracks) away from the original point then I am going in the wrong direction. The ultimate form of this navigation was the Coles sun compass used by the long range desert patrols in the Second World War. My method is rough and ready and doesn't work accurately, as the sun moves, but it is a good guide.

Navigational equipment

The following lists some of the very useful navigational equipment that is available at the present time, some highly sophisticated, some not.

Compasses

Magnetic vehicle compasses (unless you spend a great deal on them) tend to be unreliable and need a great deal of compensation for the metal, magnets and wiring in your car. There are electronic fluxgate compasses which are more accurate, but again they are expensive. I don't use either. Instead I get out of the vehicle and use my old Silva Compass that has served me superbly for the last 30 years. These stops are advantageous *per se*; they stop you driving on at great speed, allow regular breaks to regroup your party and enable you to have a look back at the way you have come (just in case you have to reverse your tracks).

LORAN

Many people in the Middle East are using ship navigation systems called LORAN. These use the radio signals from lines of transmitters to calculate position. They were intended for ships but if you are in range of the transmitters then they work perfectly well on land. The main problem with them is that the USA Department of Defence has with-drawn funding from the system and in some countries they will be switched off in the next few years.

GPS

Now that GPS have become much more easily available and affordable many people carry these in their vehicle. Some are extremely compli-cated and have numerous displays, readouts and memories for dozens of pre-entered or logged routes. Many also need sophisticated external antenna mounting on the vehicle. The main reason for these features is that they were primarily designed for boat use.

If you're going to buy a GPS, then keep it simple. It should be:
- dustproof and waterproof.
- simple to operate with a display that gives you only the essential information of:
  - where you are.
  - distance to destination.
  - bearing to destination.
  - speed over ground.
- easy to enter locations (waypoints) either before the trip or during the trip.
- able to log where you have been.
- able to run for a long time on the internal batteries and easily switchable to vehicle power.
- self contained, i.e. no external antenna required as these are easily damaged or knocked off the vehicle.
- able to transfer the display between lat/long and local grid systems.
- able to access multiple satellites at the same time for greater accuracy.

I use a small handheld Silva XL1000 which I find superb. I stick it to the dashboard with a piece of velcro tape and the only accessory needed is the vehicle power lead which plugs into the cigar lighter. It also has the advantage that it has a built in fluxgate compass, a feature that no other GPS has.

Finally, beware buying second-hand a GPS manufactured before 1996. It will probably have to be returned to the manufacturer after 1999 when the internal clock software will no longer work.

Last, and most important, never rely completely on a GPS. Like anything else, it can fail. Ensure you write down and plot on your map the route taken and all important waypoints to enable you to drive back without using the GPS.

Notebook, ruler, protractor and pencils
These are every bit as important as the rest of the equipment. They are ideally stored in a zipped document folder that will prevent them getting trampled underfoot or blown away.

Maps
Always get the best possible maps. But remember scales such as 1:50,000 tend to be too small a scale for desert navigation – you soon run off the edge of them. Far better to use one of the larger scales such as 1:100,000 or 1:250,000. Don't hesitate to supplement them with notes on the areas through which you have travelled, nor to make notes of the location and description of interesting or dominating features.

Roamers

This further piece of navigational equipment makes life a lot easier. A piece of plastic or card with the relevant grid or latitude/longitude scaling drawn on it, it enables you accurately to:

- mark your position, as given by GPS, on the map.
- estimate positions on the map for entry into a GPS or logging.

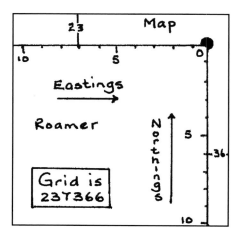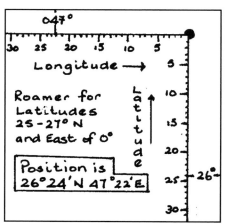

Note: Roamers based on standard scale maps do not vary anywhere in the grid system. You will however have to have separate latitude/longitude roamers for every degree that you move north or south (because of the convergence of the lines of longitude as they approach the poles).

Final Checks

Compasses: If you have a vehicle compass, has it been compensated and checked? You should still carry a hand compass and make sure you carry it as far away from the vehicle compass as possible before use.

GPS/LORAN Navigator: Is it working? Have you got spare batteries? And can you use it?

Notebook: Do you have a notebook and pencils in order to record where you have been, draw sketch maps, etc?

Maps: Have you got them all? Do you have a "roamer" to enable you accurately to plot your position on the map?

GENERAL FEATURES OF 4-WHEEL DRIVE CARS

Gearing

High gears, 2-wheel and 4-wheel drive:
This is the gearbox that is used for most road and track use. It enables the vehicle to travel at normal road speeds.

Normally, you should use high box, 2-wheel drive. Maximum speed should be limited to 120 kph because tyres are subjected to greater stress when they have been used for off-road driving and therefore have a higher risk of failure. Petrol consumption will be 35-50 kp10l.

In most cases you have to engage 4-wheel drive manually. This can usually be done at any speed but not if you are turning a corner or the vehicle's wheels are slipping. You only need 4-wheel drive when you leave the road or even good tracks, or in very slippery conditions such as mud, snow or ice.

In the new Landrovers, Range Rovers and Discoveries you are in permanent 4-wheel drive.

Low gears, 4-wheel drive:
In the low box an extra set of gears makes the engine turn at much higher revolutions for any given speed. This gives you much greater power to the wheels but limits your top speed and increases your petrol consumption.

Never engage low box whilst the vehicle is moving. You will destroy, or at least severely damage, the gearbox!

You can quite easily set off in any gear as the whole range of the gearbox is equivalent to the 1st and 2nd gears on high box.

Watch out for engine overheating. You are turning the engine over fast but the restricted forward speed can reduce the flow of air through the radiator and limit engine cooling.

Speed should not exceed 50 kph. You will get a petrol consumption of 18-26 kp10l.

Differential lock

The powered axle on a car has a gearing system called a differential. It allows one wheel to move faster than the other when cornering. The Landrover, with its permanent 4-wheel drive, has a differential on each axle and a third central differential that allows the front wheels to move at a different speed to the rear wheels. These systems are essential for on-road driving (otherwise you wear the rubber off the tyres). But unless they can be locked they put you at a disadvantage when driving in soft and slippery conditions. When you lose traction on one wheel and it slips, you lose all power to the other wheel.

The differential lock on the Landrover locks the central differential. If one set of wheels slips or loses traction you still have power to the other axle. You can engage this while travelling, but always with your wheels in a straight line and before they start slipping.

Some 4-wheel drive vehicles, especially military vehicles, have locks not only on the central differential but on each driven axle.

Brakes
Handbrake:
- Excellent since most operate on the transmission, and brake all four wheels.
- Should hold on 1-in-1 hill, i.e. 45° slope.

Ordinary Brakes:
- These are nothing like as good as the ones on your car. They are sufficient for normal road use but beware when fully loaded. They will not work as effectively in some of the steep situations that a 4-wheel drive
vehicle can get into.
- The golden rule is always go down hills in a lower gear than you went up in and use low box if necessary; this minimises your use of the brakes. (Also put the airconditioner on if you have one – these use up to 20% of the engines power and make engine braking even more effective.)
- After going through deep water, allow the brakes to dry out thoroughly.
- Finally remember that the 4-wheel drive system gives you much better road holding but does not improve braking.

Tyres
The tyres on 4-wheel drive vehicles need special care and attention. Remember that they are not road tyres, so cannot cope as well with high speed or wet conditions. They are often seriously abused by being driven hard over rocky surfaces or at low pressures over sand.

You should inspect them more frequently than you would an ordinary car and pay particular attention to pressure and any cuts or surface damage.
- It is also well worthwhile having them fitted with inner tubes. It is much easier to repair an inner tube than a tubeless tyre and you can carry more spare inner tubes.
- If you drive a lot in the desert, you should change the tyres every year.
- Ensure your puncture doesn't happen at 140 kph on the express way.
- Finally, remember that whatever you do and however well you look after your tyres, you will have more punctures than in a normal car.

Handling

Remember that the centre of gravity in a 4-wheel drive is by design much higher than in a saloon car and the vehicle itself is much heavier. This means that you cannot corner as fast because you induce more sideways roll and can therefore roll over more easily, especially if you hit an obstacle while you are cornering.

Also beware very wide desert or sand tyres on wet roads. They aquaplane readily and your stopping distance may be greatly increased.

Comfort and safety

Always remember that these vehicles are not the most comfortable in the world. You, as the driver, may be all right, but remember your poor passengers who don't have a steering wheel to hang onto and don't always see the bumps coming. This is especially true for rear seat passengers, so ensure they have adequate seat belts and make sure they use them. I have heard some desert drivers say that you shouldn't use seatbelts when driving cross-country. This is nonsense! Look at a vehicle that belongs to a real expert: not only will he have full harnesses but he will probably also have installed bucket seats.

VEHICLE PROBLEMS

This book makes no attempt to replace either a good workshop manual or a working knowledge of vehicle mechanics and repair. If you intend to go out in the desert regularly then you need to attend a specialist course on the subject – or ensure the Landrover workshop manager is in the party!

It is amazing what faults you can work around for long enough to get home or to a garage. On one occasion I drove a Landrover for 100 km with no clutch. I started the vehicle turning the engine over whilst in first gear and then I managed to change gear by ensuring the engine revs were just right. We also drove another vehicle for 50 km without any brakes – the engine was used for braking and as long as we used the gears correctly they provided sufficient braking power. You would never contemplate such measures on the road but in the desert, needs must when the devil drives.

Prevention

As stated before, it's better to get all the problems sorted out before you go out into the desert. Ensure the vehicle has been thoroughly checked and any small problems sorted out. If you have a problem with some mechanical part of the car that you know is gradually failing then, ideally, change it or at least take a spare.

Before any longer expedition make sure the vehicle is fully serviced and checked by a reputable garage and tell them what you plan to undertake. Ask them what spares you should take with you and if you don't know how to fit a part ask the mechanic to explain.

If you're out for more than one day then you should repeat your vehicle checks first thing every morning.

Most common problems

The most common problems that occur in the desert are punctures and faults due to parts, cables and leads working loose with the constant rough rides and vibrations. Accessories will often work loose and even fall off, so include an inspection of these in your daily checks.

Punctures

You will inevitably suffer from many punctures in your desert travels, especially where you are travelling over rocky terrain, or over sand with the tyres at low pressure. If you have a puncture, stop immediately. Driving for as little as 50 m on a flat tyre can so damage it as to make repair impossible. You should ideally carry two spare wheels, spare inner tubes, the equipment to repair punctures and, on long expeditions, even spare tyres (only the cover, not the whole wheel).

You will also need a reliable, and tested, heavy duty 12-volt electric air pump. It is best to have inner tubes fitted as they are easier to repair and refit (achieving the required pressure to re-seal a tubeless tyre is difficult away from a garage).

If you are forced to carry out a desert repair then here are a couple of tips:

- To get the tyre off the wheel, remove it from the vehicle, lay it on the ground and run another vehicle's wheel over the tyre part. This will force the punctured tyre away from the wheel rim and you will then be able to insert the tyre levers.
- You can buy long tubes that enable you to bleed air out of the spare tyre in order to pump up a flat tyre. This is a useful piece of kit as you have a high pressure high volume source that will easily inflate the repaired tyre and force it back onto the rim. It is then easier to re-inflate the spare using your electric pump. You can improve the air-source by over-inflating the spare, but ensure you don't exceed the manufacturer's recommendations which are usually written on the side wall of the tyre.

Equipment working loose
You should ensure you carry a good selection of spare nuts and bolts to repair or replace items that have worked loose with vibration.

Common engine faults
The following list outlines some of the more common problems that can occur with the vehicle engine (you should be able to solve them your-self). These notes are biased towards petrol engines, which overwhelmingly predominate in 4-wheel drive cars in the Middle East.

Engine will not start – headlights are bright
- Defective starter switch – tow start and replace on return.
- Defective starter solenoid – tow start and replace later.
- Starter turning but not engaging with engine (you will hear a whine as the starter turns) – tap starter with a hammer. If not effective, tow start or if necessary remove and clean bendix unit.
- Defective starter – tow start and replace, either from spares pack or on return.
- Automatic gearbox not in park or neutral – re-select.
- Some vehicles cannot be started unless the clutch is depressed.

Engine will not turn over – headlights are dim
- Battery charge very low – jump start and run engine for a while. If problem persists, check alternator/dynamo connections and ensure that fanbelt is tight.
- Starter jammed - turn engine off! Free by inserting spanner into starter gear teeth and levering or, if terrain allows, engage 2nd gear and rock vehicle backwards and forwards.

- Corroded battery terminal or loose connections – remove leads, clean and replace.
- Defective battery – if battery unserviceable, jump start and replace battery when you return.

Engine turns over slowly and will not start

- Battery charge low – jump start and run engine for a while.
- Corroded battery terminal or loose connections – remove leads, clean and replace.
- Defective battery – if battery unserviceable use jump start and replace when you return.
- Defective starter – tow start and replace, either from spares pack or on return.
- Defective engine to earth strap – clean and refit.

Engine turns over normally but will not start

- Ignition fault – remove a spark plug lead. With the lead well insulated, either by rags or a pair of insulated pliers, hold the end close to a metal part of the engine and try to start the engine.
- If no spark then:
  - check output from coil; if spark from it to high tension (HT) lead:
    - check distributor cap and rotor arm for cracks or damage. Replace or clean as necessary.
    - check each HT lead using the spark method from the coil and replace as necessary.
  - if no spark from coil to HT lead then check connections and leads, repair and replace as necessary.
- If there is a spark, then suspect a fuel problem and check:
  - you have not run out of petrol.
  - to see if engine is flooded – remove a spark plug. If the plug is wet the engine is flooded with petrol. Wait 5 minutes and try to restart. If this doesn't work, remove all spark plugs, clean, refit and try to start again.
  - fuel pumps are working – check by loosening fuel supply line and turn the engine over. If fuel spurts out (TAKE CARE) then the pumps and fuel lines are OK. If not, check lines, pumps and any filters; replace as necessary. Even if fuel is being pumped out there could still be a blockage in the carburettors. (If you find a fuel pump problem and you have no spare then you will have to tow the vehicle back.)
  - If a fuel injected engine, there could be an air lock in the fuel lines or injectors, especially after running out of fuel and refilling. Most injector systems have a valve/valves on the injector manifold that you can open and bleed the air

out of the lines.

◆ There could be a vapour lock due to the petrol vaporising in the carburettors, especially during very hot conditions and static running. Try wrapping a wet cloth around the carburettor/s to cool it/them down. If still no joy, then you may have air in the fuel lines due either to a tiny leak or a loose connection. This will probably require a garage to repair it.

◆ Carburettor operation – inspect for correct operation. Clean and reassemble as required.

Engine runs roughly

The more difficult faults to pinpoint and cure are those where the engine runs roughly with reduced power. Check all the above and also:

● the setting of the idling speed.
● the fuel mixture and choke adjusters have not worked loose.
● the fuel filters are not blocked.
● the air filter is not blocked.
● the plugs are correctly adjusted and not worn out.
● the vacuum system is free from leaks.
● ignition coil breaking down at high temperatures.

Engine overheats

● Remember to remove the radiator cap with caution, allow to cool first, then (using a cloth) open a half turn to relieve the pressure. When it has stopped venting, open carefully.
● Fan belt loose or broken – check and tighten or replace as necessary.
● Lack of coolant – check and top up as required. Check for leaks in radiator, hoses and engine. Replace or repair any failed hoses or use a proprietary engine leak sealant.
● Radiator air intake blocked – inspect and clean radiator air passages.
● Electric fans not working – if fans do not turn when engine hot, is thermostatic switch defective? If it is then hard wire fans for full time working.
● Engine fan jammed or viscous coupling defective – check operation with engine running.
● Thermostat defective – remove and see if jammed closed. Check operation by putting in boiling water to see if it opens. If defective replace or remove (note you can run without a thermostat).

Other faults

Most other faults, with the exception of replacing light bulbs and fuses, tend to be beyond the scope of this book and the average desert driver and will not be considered further.

DRIVING IN THE DESERT

Different terrain requires different driving techniques which are dealt with separately. Remember, these notes can only be a guideline. Experience is the real teacher in the desert. So take a course on desert driving and navigation, go out with experienced drivers as much as you can and ask questions.

There are some basic rules that you should always follow if you wish to drive safely and minimise the risk of accident.
- Don't drive too fast on the assumption that the road ahead is clear. This is an easy mistake to make when way off the beaten track. However just around the next bend or over the next rise you could find a herd of goats, a Mercedes water truck coming towards you or even your party leader stuck in the sand. Drive at a speed which will allow you to slow down, turn around or stop to avoid the obstacle.
- Keep a safe distance from the vehicle in front. A "safe distance" is difficult to quantify but the following will show possible dangers. Particular attention should be paid to this in the following situations:
  - ◆ Driving along dusty tracks. Ensure you stay far enough back to avoid the dust cloud but not so far that you lose the vehicle in front. In these circumstances the leader should stop regularly, and at every major track junction, to allow the party to regroup.
  - ◆ Driving through soft sand. In the worst conditions only one vehicle should move at a time. Here the leader should drive to firm ground in view of the rest of the party so that he can wave them on one at a time. If you all drive together and the lead vehicle gets stuck, those following may not be able to avoid the lead vehicle without getting stuck themselves.
  - ◆ Driving in convoys on roads. Most trips start and end with a long trip on the tarmac. Be alert, keep at least 100 metre spacings between vehicles and watch the vehicle behind so that you can stop or slow down when it does. This way the group will stay together. It is best to put the slowest vehicle at the front of the convoy.
- Driving off-road at night should be avoided at all costs. Tracks that in the daylight are well defined become virtually undetectable in the headlights. In the day time you can see the direction you are travelling by reference to the landscape around you. At night, without this facility, you can easily become hopelessly lost.
- Driving around midday under a vertical sun is dangerous. The sun casts no shadow and most definition of the ground is lost. You can no longer clearly see dangerous holes, slopes or other pitfalls. Best find some shade and relax until later in the day.

Desert tracks

You should normally run along hard desert tracks with the tyres at normal or even slightly (about 5 psi) higher than normal pressures. Use 2-wheel drive – be careful of harsh braking on the loose surface. Instead use cadence braking where you repeatedly and gently pump the brakes, releasing the pressure before the tyres lose grip. Also approach bends and crests slowly. There may very well be a Mercedes water truck in the middle of the track.

Corrugations

All too often you will find yourself on badly corrugated tracks (sometimes called washboard). The correct technique is to find a speed which seems to iron the bumps out (normally 50 to 70 kph). If you go any faster the rear end is liable to break away unexpectedly or the tyres will overheat and cause a blow out. Ensure you're in 2-wheel drive, with the differential locks off. This puts less strain on the central and front differentials.

Dust

Very often driving along tracks raises vast clouds of dust which makes it impossible for the vehicle behind to follow you closely. Under these circumstances ensure that you keep a good distance between vehicles but make sure you don't lose the vehicle behind. Pre-arrange to stop and re-group say every 4 km, or at major track junctions.

Also, beware of pockets of light dust which has the consistency of talcum powder (in the Middle East it tends to be much lighter in colour). Hit this at speed and you instantly raise a cloud of dust that can block air vents as well as leave an impenetrable wall which the following vehicles can't see through.

Ruts

Some tracks (especially soft or sandy ground) can become badly rutted. If your wheels run into these ruts you lose steering control. It is all too easy to oversteer, with the possible result that you suddenly break out of the ruts and rush off at 45 degrees to the track. The best solution is to reduce your speed and try to straddle the ruts so that your wheels don't run into them.

Also, beware of hard objects in the middle of the tracks – if your wheels are in the ruts you are more likely to hit the axle differential.

Rocky terrain

Go slowly.

Be wary of rocks being thrown up and damaging the underside of the vehicle or the suspension being damaged through overwork.

The only way you'll get stuck is if you try to cross something too big or deep and the underside of the vehicle or the differentials get stuck on the obstacle.

There are different ways of approaching different obstacles on rocky terrain but remember – if an obstacle is bigger than the body clearance you won't get over it.

Bumps, changes in level or dykes

Go over with both wheels together on the obstacle. This keeps the vehicle axle – the point of minimum clearance – level. For formidable obstacles use low box with differential lock and 1st gear.

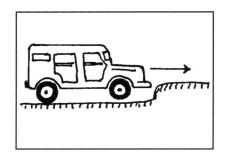

Also remember to note which side the differential is situated and avoid going over bumps on this side.

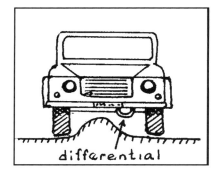

Ditches

Go across at an angle if they are deep or steep-sided. This way you only put one wheel in at a time. If both wheels go in, it's like trying to drive up a brick wall, whether you're going backwards or forwards. If only one wheel is in, the other three will pull or push you out.

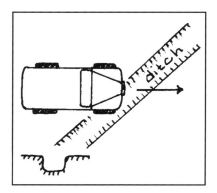

V-shaped gullies

Ensure you put your wheels either side of a v-shaped gully or the deep ruts typical of washed out tracks. Try to keep the wheels at the same height and the vehicle level.

Steep cross tracks

Most 4-wheel drives can drive up or down 45° slopes but can only lean sideways to about 25°! So when you have to drive across a steep hillside be extra careful:

- Drive slowly.
- Keep the downhill wheels out of holes.
- Keep the uphill wheels off bumps.
- Unload the roof-rack or redistribute weight as necessary. Four people hanging off the uphillside of the roof-rack balances you quite well!

Steep downhill

- Engage low gear before it gets steep.
- On the steepest downhill, 1st gear in the low box is required.
- Engage the differential lock.
- Put the airconditioning on full as this further brakes the engine.
- Let the clutch out.
- Take both feet off the pedals (don't ride the clutch and brake). Let the engine do the braking.
- Steer straight downhill – not across the slope or you'll slip or even roll over. If you start slipping sideways accelerate slightly and straighten up.

Steep Uphill

- Engage low gear before it gets steep.
- On the steepest hills 1st gear in the low box is required.
- Engage the differential lock.
- Turn off the airconditioning.

Water

- Ensure you can wade through the water, that it is no deeper than half a metre and has a good firm bottom to provide traction for the vehicles.
- Cover the radiator grill with a waterproof cover. The plastic screen shades are ideal for this. Alternatively, remove the fan belt. Either measure will help to prevent water coming through the radiator and splashing all over the engine and electrics.

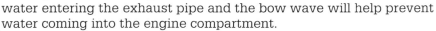

- If you have any WD40, spray it over the electrics.
- Engage low box 1st gear and drive forward fast enough to create a bow wave (about a normal walking pace). The high revs of the engine will stop water entering the exhaust pipe and the bow wave will help prevent water coming into the engine compartment.
- Do not slow down or the bow wave will collapse and the water will rush into the engine compartment
- Do not go too fast or you will force water into the engine compartment
- If you're still worried about the crossing, attach a tow-rope to the lead vehicle's rear bumper. Pay the rope out whilst you're driving across. This can then be used as a safety line for the second vehicle which should also have a tow-rope attached to the rear. This way every vehicle has at least one tow-rope attached whilst it is crossing.
- The best drivers should cross first and last.
- When you've all crossed, refit the fan belts, remove any radiator covers and allow the brakes to dry.
- Crossing deep water is the only good time to be carrying plenty of weight as it will help to keep the vehicle from floating! (They don't float for long – just enough for you to drift into deeper water before you sink!).

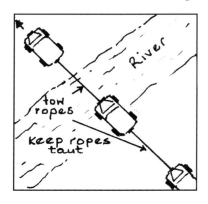

Mud

Mud should be avoided whenever possible. It is most difficult, and dirty, to recover from. If you cannot drive around mud, *recce* the route first. Ensure that the brown mess in front of you doesn't hide a river or a stream that will inevitably be deeper than its surroundings. Only commit one vehicle at a time and go through it in 4-wheel drive, low box, high gear (4th normally) and fairly fast – 30-40 kph. If it is a short section put material such as wood or vegetation into the mud first to aid traction. Don't use sand ladders unless you are forced to – it is unlikely you will find them again. It is a good idea to attach a tow-rope to the vehicle before it goes across, in the same way as you would to cross water.

Sabkha

Sabkha is the Arabian term for a salt marsh or pan which is covered by a thin, salty crust. It is often darker than the surrounding area and can sometimes look like dried foam. If there are vehicle tracks across it they will have formed deep ruts. It is most often found near the coast but any area where the water table is close to the surface can harbour this most treacherous of all surfaces.

The general rule is to avoid crossing *sabkha* at all costs. It is totally unpredictable. You can easily break through the thin dry layer and sink into the ooze beneath. (Indeed, the Bedu in the Eastern Region of Saudi Arabia tell stories of whole vehicles sinking into the *sabkha* near the coast and finally re-emerging in the Emirates!) Driving fast can be dangerous. Breaking through the surface will immediately and violently bring your vehicle to a stop while the contents carry on at 80 kph. If you have to cross, then *recce* on foot first. Look at any existing tracks – the Bedu normally know the safest and driest way across. Drive at a reasonable speed of about 30 kph in 4-wheel drive with all differential locks engaged. Only commit one vehicle at a time.

Wadi sand

You find this mix of loose sand and gravel in the bottom of wadis. It normally makes for good comfortable driving as it doesn't get rutted like the dirt tracks. But it can be soft, and after rain it can form strange changes in level that are often difficult to see (especially any fall in level).

- Beware of soft patches, unexpected holes and changes of level.
- Use 4-wheel drive high box 2nd or 3rd gear with the differential lock on. Drive fairly quickly (30-40 kph) thus using the vehicle's momentum to get through any soft bits.
- If the people behind or in front are stuck, don't stop in the wadi. Drive to hard ground and then go back to them on foot.

Sand dunes

The unpredictability of sand dunes can also cause problems. Some sand is very firm, especially after rain, but it can be a mere crust with hours of digging lurking underneath since it can hide patches of liquid sand that you drop into. Always try to choose a route that takes you through the largest but most gently sloping dunes.

- The general rule is 4-wheel drive, high box, differential lock on, 1st or 2nd gear. Keep your speed up to about 35 kpm and travel along the bottoms of the dunes. Also ensure you let your tyres down to the emergency soft pressures in the handbook to give you extra flotation on the sand. If you cannot find these then try 20 psi front and 25 psi rear – the tyres should bulge appreciably at the correct pressure for sand driving. However when you return to rock or gravel, remember to pump the tyres up or drive below 50 kpm.
- Avoid the small dunes (2-3 m high) that you often find at the edge of large dunes. They are often soft and because they are close together you cannot get up sufficient speed to cross between them safely.
- If you stop make sure it is on very firm ground. Or ensure you are facing downhill with sufficient run out to build up the speed necessary to drive on.
- If have to stop on the sand then do so slowly. A fierce application of the brakes will cause the wheels to dig in.
- When you have to restart try 2nd gear in high box with the minimum of engine revs in order keep the wheels from losing traction and spinning.
- Avoid hitting the clumps of vegetation that are sometimes found on the dunes. The roots of the plants bind the sand together to form a solid, immovable lump that will make most 4-wheel drives bounce in the air.
- Try not to follow directly in the tracks of the vehicle in front. It has probably broken through the top crust of sand to the softer stuff below.
- Avoid the steep slip sides of large dunes. As well as being steeper, the sand is looser since it is not as wind packed as the gentler slope.

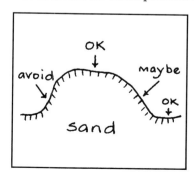

- Follow the gentlest slopes, even though this means you're rarely driving in a straight line

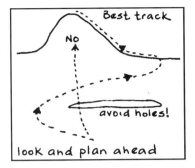

- Approach steep bits in the gear you will cross them in (normally 1st or 2nd gear, high box). Accelerate all the way over them. Hesitate, brake, or take your foot off the accelerator and you'll get stuck! Never change gear on a steep section – only on the flat or downhill! Remember, it's the vehicle's momentum that will carry it up soft steep bits so don't go too slowly. Never drive down a steep dune at an angle or you'll slip sideways. If this happens, point the vehicle straight down and accelerate out of the bottom.

- If you find yourself in a bowl or between two steep sided hills or dunes, drive around in circles gradually getting higher or run from one slope to the other gradually getting higher until you cross the obstacle.

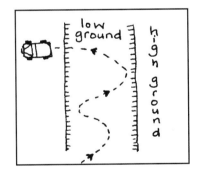

- If you have to cross the crest of a dune first, find the best descent by driving parallel for a short distance or by a *recce*. Always cross at right-angles, never at a slant, or you can lose traction as opposing wheels are left in the air.

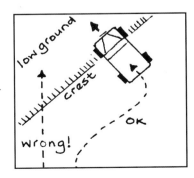

Finally, remember that sand dunes shift and change shape in the wind, sometimes at an alarming rate. Just because the ascent of a dune looks good (there may even be vehicle tracks disappearing over the summit) this does not guarantee the descent: the wind may well have hollowed out the other side.

Sand dunes seem to bring out the cowboy in many of us, so take care. If in doubt, do a *recce* on foot

Automatics

If you have an automatic gearbox, usually the low box is geared much higher than the manual version. This means the following:

- You will not get as much engine braking when going down hills, even when you are in low box and locked in 1st gear.
- You will need to go into low box sooner than in a manual, especially for going up or down steep hills.
- On sand you should be in low box, normally locked in 3rd gear. Here you are at a advantage over manually geared vehicles as you can change gear without losing power to the wheels.
- Don't allow the vehicle to idle for long periods in the park position
- If you have a winch fitted then do not engage park when you use it. You could damage the transmission.

SOME FINAL DO'S AND DON'TS

- Do not use 4-wheel drive or differential lock on dry tarmac roads or good tracks. This wears out your tyres at an alarming rate.
- Do not wrap your thumbs around the steering wheel. If you hit a bad bump, the wheel can be wrenched sideways and break your thumbs.
- Never engage the low gearbox whilst you're moving.
- Do not engage the handbrake on a moving vehicle. You will probably lock all 4 wheels and lose control.
- Always engage 4-wheel drive and differential lock **before** you get into trouble and the wheels start to lose traction.
- If in doubt, get out and walk the route first.
- Only ever attempt what your experience, your vehicle and equipment are capable of.

RECOVERY TECHNIQUES

Remember the golden rules of recovery:
- Try not to get stuck in the first place. Always walk a difficult piece of terrain first and, if you have to, drive around the obstacle. An extra three kilometres of driving is better than than two hours of digging!
- Never commit all your vehicles. If one of three vehicles gets stuck let one other attempt to help it. That way, if the recovering vehicle gets stuck as well, you've still got one vehicle in which you can drive out.
- If the chassis of your vehicle is resting on the ground, you're stuck. You will not move until you have removed the obstacle or lifted the vehicle off it.
- Ensure only one person is in charge of the whole procedure. He should be the most experienced at recovery. Having two people giving instructions is a recipe for disaster and serious injury. Also ensure one of the best drivers gets in the vehicle to be recovered. Don't be macho and try to do it all yourself. Even the best of us have been stuck and have accepted help.

Towing on roads (see also page 45)
If you have to tow a vehicle back home by road, follow these few basic rules:
- Use the largest, most powerful vehicle to do the towing.
- Make sure the vehicle being towed has its steering unlocked and engine running in order to give power to the brakes and steering. If the vehicle's engine has stopped, don't attempt a long tow. Seek a proper recovery vehicle.
- Make sure the vehicle being towed is out of gear and in the neutral setting between high and low gearboxes.
- Use a short (8 m) tow-rope with some elasticity to avoid the sudden jerks of braking and starting up.
- The vehicle being towed must do the braking for both.
- The tow-rope should be kept taut at all times. Beware of the normal reaction to over-brake as you don't appear to be stopping as fast as you normally would.
- The towing vehicle should not exceed 50 kph.
- If your car is recovered by a professional tow-truck with your front wheels suspended in the air, make sure that you are in neutral if your car is selectable 2/4-wheel drive. If the vehicle is permanent 4-wheel drive, remove the front prop-shaft.

Rocky terrain

If you're bogged in, it's probably your fault – you've either tried to cross an obstacle that is too big or you've not approached something correctly. It's better to drive an extra kilometre than get stuck.

Don't attempt to pull the vehicle out if it's grounded on rocks. All you'll do is badly damage the underside. You must jack the vehicle up and build the ground up under the wheels until you can drive off. You can use strong sand ladders as bridges over big drops or holes.

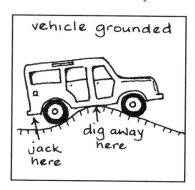 

Water
If you stop in water :
- You will normally have to be pulled out. You should have attached the tow-rope before starting the crossing, because the towing point will now be at least a foot under water.
- A method of self-recovery if the engine has stopped and won't restart is to put the vehicle into 1st or reverse gear in the low gearbox and engage the starter. This will turn the engine over and slowly "wind" the vehicle out without the engine having to start! Most good batteries will cope with at least 100 m of this! Do not attempt this if the water is over the air intake. You will suck water into the engine and severely damage the valves and camshaft.

Mud
If you are stuck in mud you will have to build a roadway and/or be winched out. The mud clinging to the underside of the vehicle can form a vacuum that prevents normal towing. Snatch tows can be dangerous at the pull required may be so great that shackles and anchor points fail.

The easiest solution is to dig the mud away from the wheels and put vegetation, sacks or pieces of wood down to give the wheels a grip. (You can use sand ladders but they have a disconcerting habit of disappearing.)

Next winch the vehicle out, or if you don't have a winch, use two vehicles pulling at the same time, or a snatch block to increase the power of the pull. (See page 46.)

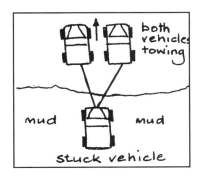 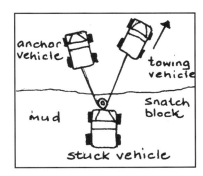

Sand

Again, the first rule is not to get stuck. If you're not happy about a stretch of dunes then walk it first. Only stop your vehicle facing downhill and on more solid ground.

Some of the situations you will encounter are as follows:

Stuck going uphill: Reverse back down slowly using the engine and keeping the wheels in a straight line until you're on easier ground.

Stuck on the top of a crest: This normally happens if you've hesitated at the last moment of crossing or have tried the manoeuvre too slowly. The only reliable way off is to dig out all the sand until all four wheels again have traction and the vehicle chassis is no longer resting on the sand. You can pull the vehicle off with another 4-wheel drive but this can damage the underneath of the vehicle especially exposed brake pipes.

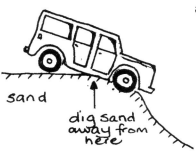 

Stuck crossing a steep slope: This normally happens when you've tried to get up a slope, realised it's not possible and waited too long before turning back down the slope. Sand has piled up against the downhill wheels, you're going nowhere and you are leaning at an appalling angle down the hill. Dig away the sand from the front wheels to enable you to turn them to full lock pointing down the hill. Then drive very slowly downhill with everyone pushing the front of the vehicle down the hill. Once you

have traction gradually straighten the front wheels and drive to better ground. This is always a dangerous situation and you should avoid getting on the downhill side of the vehicle in case it turns over.

Stuck on the flat or in a bowl: This can take a long time if you're stuck badly. First stop and fully assess the situation. Don't keep churning away in the same spot: you're only digging yourself in deeper! Work out in which direction to move the vehicle. Always try to move down any slope if possible, but not if this will cause further problems.

- Stop, get out and clear the sand from in front of the wheels. You will see it builds up into a little mound. If you are not in too deep, that's all you need to clear. If you've got one wheel in deeply you can drag it along. Move forward as slowly as you can: 2nd gear, low box, differential lock on, minimum revs. With everyone pushing you should be able to move forwards a few feet until the sand builds up again. Then repeat the process.

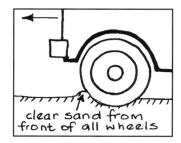

- If this doesn't work try digging the sand out from in front of the wheels to make a ramp. Again crawl forward with everyone pushing. Don't allow a half-hearted effort. Make sure that all the sand is removed. If you haven't done so already, let the tyres down to the emergency soft pressures.

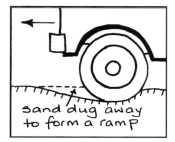

● A technique that often works is to distribute your party on either side of the vehicle and rock it from side to side as violently as you can. This lifts the vehicle wheels out of the sand faster than any other method but it only works if the chassis is clear of the sand.

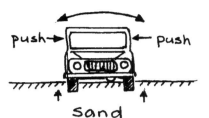

● The next stage is to put something under the wheels to increase their grip. Ideally use sand ladders, but if you do not have any (mistake!) use old sacks, vegetation, car mats or, best of all, rocks. Again drive forwards in 2nd gear, low box, differential lock on.

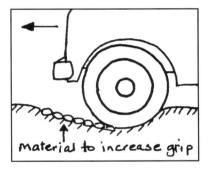

● If none of these techniques work then jack the vehicle up and fill in the gaps under the wheels with sand or stones. Then put your sand ladders under the wheels.

Remember, you'll need a wooden board under thejack to stop it sinking into the sand or better still, use an air bag jack which is ideal on soft sand. If you can't lift the vehicle out of the sand in one go then fill in the space under the wheels and start jacking again.

Then crawl out of the sand, 2nd gear, low box, differential lock on and minimum revs again with every one pushing. If necessary move the sand ladders quickly in front of the wheels again to create a sort of rolling road.

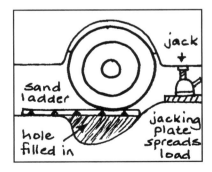

If it's so soft as to be undriveable, then you'll have continue doing this until you reach firm ground or somewhere where you can be pulled out with a winch or tow vehicle.

● The most embarrassing situation you can find yourself in is when your vehicle has rolled over onto its side – more frequent in the sand than you would think. First, ensure the vehicle is made safe by disconnecting and removing the battery (beware of spilled battery acid) and covering spilled petrol with sand. Then, with fire extinguishers at the ready, remove all the equipment from the vehicle and roof rack. Next dig small holes about 30 cm deep underneath the wheels nearest to the ground. This will allow the vehicle to roll back more easily. Now attach a tow-rope to the chassis at the top. With everyone pushing, tow the vehicle on to its wheels.

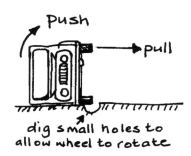

push

pull

dig small holes to allow wheel to rotate

Now sort out the mess. Pull the vehicle out of the holes you dug. Check all the fluid levels and top up as necessary. Repack the vehicle. Most times the vehicle is really no worse for wear except for a few scratches and dents.

TOWING AND WINCHING

First, all towing and winching is potentially dangerous as ropes do snap and anchor points break. Ensure everyone is clear of the area and only one person is in control. His job is to ensure everyone is clear before vehicles start to move.

EQUIPMENT

Wire Cables
A short wire cable is ideal for use on road and in rocky terrain where you've got a good surface to grip on. Don't snatch at the towrope or it's liable to break. These are also used on powered winches (except capstan winches).

Nylon Ropes
Each vehicle should have two nylon or polypropalene ropes, one 8 m length and one 25 m length (if you've got four vehicles each with these lengths of rope then you can tow from 100 m away). The problem with these ropes is that they are very easily cut, melt at just over 300°C and will dissolve if exposed to petrol, acid or grease. So don't just throw them in the back of the vehicle and don't let them get near a hot exhaust. I don't try to coil my tow-rope – instead I just feed it into a large plastic bag. It never gets knotted up and it's protected from oils etc. The ends should have loops spliced into them. This hardly reduces the breaking strain; knots, on the other hand, can reduce the strength by up to 50% and are impossible to untie after being pulled tight.

Snatch Ropes
Snatch ropes, sometimes called kinetic energy recovery ropes (KERR), are used differently from all other tow-ropes in that the towing vehicle accelerates away from the stuck vehicle. The rope stretches out, converting the momentum of the moving vehicle into potential energy in the rope which will pop the stuck vehicle out of the sand. They should not be used where the vehicle is stuck on rocks or solid objects as the energies generated can easily damage the bottom of the vehicle as it is pulled off.

Winches
Winches are mechanical devices that can be used slowly to pull vehicles out of obstacles or up steep hills or even to lower down steep hills. They can be permanently fitted to the vehicle, usually on the front bumper, and are normally powered electrically. Some older Landrovers have a superb mechanical capstan winch powered directly from the engine using a separate winch rope wrapped around the capstan. There are also portable winches that can be

attached to anywhere on the vehicle (or any immovable object such as a tree or a large rock). Some are electrically powered with a long fly-lead to run from the car battery and some, such as Tirfor winches, are hand powered.

Other equipment you will also need:

- Several (I normally carry six) large shackles to join ropes together or attach them to the vehicle. These must be appreciably stronger than the rope – far better the rope breaks and flies through the air than a large steel shackle. Check that your shackles fit into the towing point of your vehicle.
- Gloves, which are essential for handling steel cables.
- Two or three short strops (loops of rope or nylon tape ideally stronger than the tow-rope) that you can use with a shackle to attach snatch blocks or tow-ropes to vehicles that do not have towing brackets or eyes.
- A snatch block. This is a large pulley that you can attach to an anchor point and pass the tow-rope through. This is an extremely useful and relatively inexpensive piece of equiment that allows you to double the power of a tow or tow from different angles.

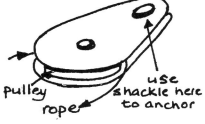

- Ideally, front and rear tow-hooks or at least strong towing points fitted to the vehicle. Many of the hooks and rings that are found under neath vehicles are designed for tying the vehicle down during transportation, not for towing or winching. Please note this is especially true for snatch tows where the energy generated can rip off weaker anchorage points.

Techniques

The following sections will illustrate the main techniques but they are not exhaustive. When presented with a situation where you need to tow or winch a little time spent considering the problem will always pay dividends. Be very careful in how you attach the rope to the vehicles. Don't wrap it around a bumper and tie it on. If you do, the sharp edges will cut the rope.

Use tow-hooks and shackles or a separate wire/strop around the chassis (not the bumper as it's not unknown for bumpers to be recovered before the rest of the vehicle).

If you have to shorten a rope, then loop it completely around, i.e. double it up. If you tie a knot in it and put it under strain the knot will never undo.

Many of the techniques are common to both towing and winching.

Basic tows

The towing or winching vehicle should be on solid ground and ideally in line with the vehicle to be recovered.

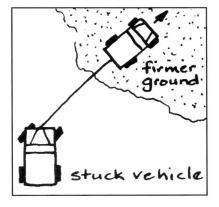

You can tow at an angle but then only from the front of the stuck vehicle whose front wheels must be turned to be in line with the tow. Both vehicles should be in low box, differential locks engaged. Pull at a crawling speed. It is essential that the stuck vehicle attempts to drive out to help the tow. The only time that its advantageous for the vehicle to free-wheel is if you are winching it in soft sand onto sand ladders. In this case allowing it to be pulled will stop it digging deeper into the sand and allow it to ride up on to the sand ladders. You can double the pulling power by using a snatch block attached to the vehicle being recovered. The tow- or winch-rope is threaded through the snatch block and attached either to the winching vehicle or, if towing, to another anchor point.

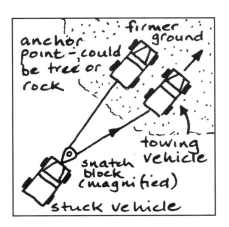

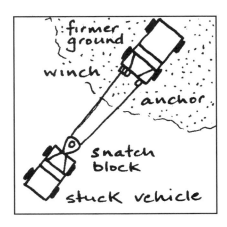

Towing over a rise in the ground

Remember you need good firm ground for the towing vehicle. In some circumstances you may have to join all your tow-ropes together and tow from a long way off. Be careful, however, not to let the tow-rope run over the top of a sand dune or rock as it will break. If you are forced to cross a rise in the ground put a vehicle with a snatch block attached at the high point and run the rope through it.

If necessary you can then recover this second vehicle by towing or winching.

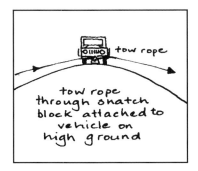

Towing or winching at an angle

Sometimes it is impossible to pull the vehicle out in a straight line, as there is just no suitable ground. In these circumstances a snatch block is extremely useful. Place another vehicle in a straight line with the one to be recovered, attach the snatch block to it and run the tow or winch cable through it. You then pull the vehicle to be recovered towards the vehicle with the snatch block. Once it is in line with the recovery vehicle you can recover (both if necessary) with a direct pull.

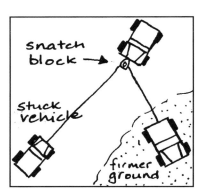

Snatch tows

This is a very useful recovery technique for soft sand, especially if the vehicle is stuck in a patch of soft sand next to a good track or in a small bowl. However, remember this is potentially a dangerous procedure that should only be carried out by experienced drivers using properly constructed kinetic energy recovery ropes (KERR). Short safety strops should be used in addition to secure the shackles in case of failure. The inherent dangers of this procedure cannot be overstated. A 10 pound towing bracket flying off at your windscreen is a scary sight!

Straight snatch tow

If you have good firm ground nearby reverse the towing vehicle as close to the stuck vehicle as possible and attach the snatch rope to both. The rope should be carefully arranged on the ground between the two vehicles to avoid it tying itself in knots as it tightens. The towing vehicle then accelerates away at 15 or 25 kph. The rope stretches out and you convert all the momentum of the towing vehicle into tension. Out pops the stuck vehicle.

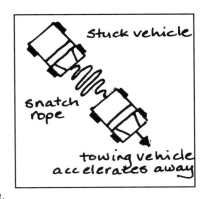

Snatch tow in a bowl

Another use for these ropes is if a vehicle is stuck in a bowl or a dip in the sand. It is very difficult to tow out directly and if you start the towing vehicle in the bowl, it is likely to get stuck as well. Here the towing vehicle starts at the top of the bowl and drives down and past the vehicle being re-covered and up the other side. Great care has to be taken with how you lay out the rope to ensure it doesn't snag on either vehicle.

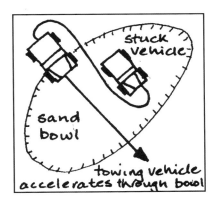

Note: With both these techniques it is often advantageous to make a pathway of sand ladders for the towing vehicle to give it better grip.

Sand ladders

Each vehicle should have a set of these invaluable tools. Sand ladders are short sections of light steel ladder, usually at least about 1m long and 25 cm wide and they should have a rung every 20 cm to give traction to the vehicle wheels. You can find shorter ones on the market or ones with very widely spaced rungs but they are of little value. There are also excellent aluminium ladders where short sections are joined by rope. They should have have 1.5 m lengths of cord attached to them to enable you to find them when they have buried themselves in the sand.

It is also a good idea to mark their position before use with sticks or shovels in the sand close by. This will help you to find the ladders after recovering the vehicle.

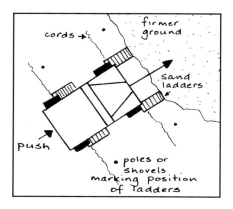
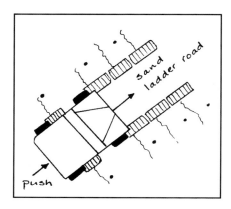

Sand ladders are mainly used when you're on really soft sand. You can put them under your wheels and form a solid path. If all the vehicles have them you can put them all out and make a sand ladder road out of the sand by moving the ones you have gone over round to the front of the vehicle. Often it's easier to use them under the towing vehicle to give it the required traction to pull the other vehicle out (as you can drive the towing vehicle onto the channels). Other uses are getting down short deep drops, across deep holes or gullies or as BBQ's.

SURVIVAL TECHNIQUES

There are many good books which deal in great detail with desert survival and I make no attempt to emulate them. I am sure there are lots of delicious plants and animals, but for the majority of people they will not be necessary, as rescue will come within a couple of days. The following points should be sufficient:

Single vehicle problems

If one vehicle breaks down or becomes inextricably stuck, you may be forced to leave it behind. In these circumstances, move the people and their food, water, any safety equipment and valuables into your other vehicles and abandon the trip. Lock the vehicle you're leaving behind and put a note on it saying what your route, plans and timings are. Then drive out by the safest and easiest route – often this is by reversing your tracks. You can always come back later with more help to recover the vehicle.

Problems affecting the whole party

If all your vehicles get stuck or break down, don't panic. Remember the following:
- You have been sensible and are well prepared.
- You have left your route and timings with a friend and he will telephone the police to alert the rescue organisations when you don't return.
- You have plenty of water to last several days.
- After a rest, and in the cool of the morning, you may be able to extract the stuck vehicle(s). This is especially true on sand where the early morning dew makes the sand much firmer and easier to drive on.

Your priority actions are as follows:
- Whatever happens do not leave your vehicles. *They* will be found. If you leave them, the chances are *you* will not!
- Erect some shade. You can use a tarpaulin or plastic sheet spread between the vehicles. Try to capture any cooling breezes.
- Immediately ration your food and water supplies – remember there is about a gallon in each vehicle's windscreen washer bottle. Do not drink the vehicle coolant as this invariably contains poisonous antifreeze.
- If you have a 2-way radio or mobile telephone go to the highest ground close by and try calling the emergency services. If you're a long way from civilisation this may not work but it's well worth trying. Remember to hold the antenna vertically to maximise the range.
- If you have a search and rescue radio beacon (SARBE), turn it on.
- Put out marker panels on the ground in the shape of a cross. Erect

poles with flags on them (coloured cloth or plastic) on the tops of surrounding high ground. Write a large "help" on the ground with stones.

- Prepare a signal fire, for daytime use, either with local wood and engine oil or a spare tyre (remember to deflate it first). Get a mirror out so you can quickly use it to signal to search planes or vehicles. Don't bother trying to spell out "SOS" in morse as repeated flashing will alert them just as well.
- Tune your radio into a local station and listen to the news broadcasts.
- If you start to get too hot, and have a vehicle that's still working, get in it and switch the air conditioning on for a while. Beware, however, of overheating the engine and of exhaust fumes.
- At night leave a light or torch on – one that flashes is best – and if you hear a plane or vehicle turn on your headlights and 4 way flashers.
- Carry out any strenuous work at night or in the morning when it is cooler.
- Relax, wait and don't panic – someone will come along sooner than you think.

Solar stills

The solar still is one effective water collection technique, especially if the sand is damp underneath or there are abundant plants close by. Dig a pit in the ground or sand where it is dampest (this is normally in a hollow in the sand or a dry river bed). Put urine and crushed vegetation in the bottom of the pit and a container in the middle to catch the water. Cover this with a clear plastic sheet which is anchored down securely all around the edges and has a stone on top of it to make an inverted cone, the point of which is directly over the water collection container.

The sun heats up the ground and vegetation and any moisture in it evaporates. The moisture then condenses on the inside of the plastic sheet and drips into the container. Using this technique I have managed to collect over half a litre in a couple of hours. Remember to resupply the vegetation or, if you are using damp ground, move the still. This is a method that you should practise before you get stuck!

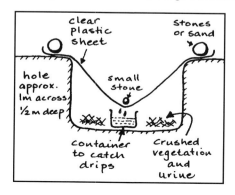

FIRST AID IN A DESERT ENVIRONMENT

Some notes by Dr John G Gibbons – based on the Middle East. For hazards in other areas talk to the local medical services.

Accident prevention
The planning of a trip to the desert should involve the minimisation of risk. Most accidents are unforeseen but it is possible to plan ahead. Consider what hazards are likely to be encountered and what measures can be taken beforehand to lessen the risk. Important factors include:
- Number of people in the group.
- State of health of these people.
- Duration of the trip.
- Travelling time to nearest medical facility.
- Time of year/conditions to be encountered.
- Experience, including medical experience of group members.

It is important that a first aid kit is available. The contents will depend on the uses to which it may be put and the level of training of those who may use it.

Do not forget to keep your first aid kit in a place that is easy to reach. The best place is somewhere in the middle of the vehicle where it is less likely to be damaged in an accident.

Hazards
The practice of first aid in a desert environment differs little from that of any other environment, except for some health hazards that are specific to the desert. It is possible to break down these hazards, but the desert environment will have an impact in the following areas:
- Management of pre existing medical conditions.
- General accidents involving cuts, abrasions and burns.
- Injuries from harmful desert plants, insects and animals.
- Injuries sustained due to exposure to heat.
- Sandstorms.
- Food poisoning.

In the management of pre-existing medical problems consider the following factors:
- The general state of health of those venturing into the desert.
- Level of fitness: is the person capable of assisting in heavy manual work in a hot environment?
- Will regular prescribed medication be heat stable? For example,

consideration must be given to the storage of insulin for an insulin-dependent diabetic. The time of year and the length of the trip must be taken into account.

- If a person suffers from severe allergies, should they be venturing into a hostile environment away from medical facilities?
- Although it is safe to bring young children to the desert is it wise to take them on a long trip over several days?
- Remember to store any required medicines in a cool place away from direct sunlight and in a part of the vehicle that is easily accessible.

Treatment of cuts, lacerations and abrasions
- Wash the area with an antiseptic solution. Don't forget that freshly voided urine is usually sterile and is perfectly acceptable for use as a wound cleanser. It is certainly preferable to a contaminated water source.
- If bleeding is brisk, apply pressure to the area and elevate.
- If there are trained personnel present with the appropriate equip ment suturing may be attempted. If not apply a firm clean dressing. If the wound is serious transport to a medical facility immediately.

Burns
Burns often occur in the desert as a result of campfire and cooking accidents or even just touching bare metal surfaces in summer. Many of these injuries can be prevented by the use of gloves, even in summer. Their treatment is as follows:

1st degree burns: involve the outer layer of skin only with redness of the skin but no blistering.
- Wash with cool water immediately.
- Dress with Flamazine cream if available. If not apply a moist gauze bandage.

2nd degree burns: involve damage to deeper layers of the skin, i.e. the dermis (the characteristic sign of 2nd degree burns is blistering).
- Wash with cool water if the blisters have not burst. If they have, use an antiseptic solution.
- Cover with an antiseptic cream.
- Apply a dry dressing.
- Give pain relief.

3rd degree burns: these are the most serious and involve damage to the subcutaneous tissues.
- Apply a dry dressing.
- Bandage loosely.
- Seek medical help immediately.

HARMFUL PLANTS, INSECTS AND ANIMALS

General precautions
- Use an insect repellent.
- Wear protective clothing, particularly boots that protect the ankles.
- Do not reach under rocks or put your hands into areas where insects/scorpions/snakes may be lurking.
- Sleep off the ground.
- Shake out boots and clothing in the morning before putting them on.
- Do not approach wild animals.
- Keep children under supervision.
- Avoid touching unfamiliar plants, especially those with milky sap.

Plants
There are few really poisonous desert plants but avoid any that are not eaten by the local animals and any that have a white milky sap.
- Use gloves when you handle any unfamiliar or known poisonous plants.
- If you get any sap on your skin wash it off as soon as possible.

Insect and spider bites
Avoid insect bites by camping away from water or locally populated sites. Wear long sleeved shirts, long trousers tucked into your socks and a liberal application of insect repellent. If you do get bitten, clean with an antiseptic solution and dress with an antiseptic ointment. The same advice holds true for spider bites.

Ticks are occasionally encountered and they may attach themselves to the skin. They are best removed by applying an irritant chemical or direct heat, i.e. the heat of a lighted cigarette tip – applied to the tick with great care! Subsequently the injury is treated as above for insect bites.

Snake bites
Thankfully snakes are encountered infrequently in the desert. If someone is bitten:
- Lie the victim down.
- Keep calm and reassure the victim.
- Wash the bite area with water or an antiseptic solution.
- If practical, apply a constricting bandage above the site of the bite, between the bite and the heart. The object is to restrict lymphatic flow – the constriction should not be so tight as to restrict the arterial blood flow.
- Do not give the victim anything by mouth.
- Immobilise the area affected.

- Treat for shock if necessary.
- If possible, kill the snake and bring it with you. As it may be possible to identify it and administer the appropriate antivenom later.
- Seek medical help.

Scorpion stings
These should be treated in a similar way to snake bites.
Remember: Scorpions are nocturnal creatures and they seek out hiding places at daybreak.

Mosquitoes
Malaria is not a major concern in Saudi Arabia or the Gulf. The central, eastern and northern areas are risk free. Mountainous areas are also safe. The risk areas are those bordering Yemen. Remember mosquitoes tend to be found close to stagnant water so avoid these areas. Ask locally to assess the risk in your area.

Precautions:
- Use an insect repellent.
- Seek local advice on the need to take preventive treatment for malaria.
- Treat mosquito bites with antiseptic solution and an antihistamine cream to control itching.

DISORDERS ASSOCIATED WITH EXCESSIVE EXPOSURE TO HEAT
(Sources include SAS Survival Manual)

Overview:
The desert environment exposes you to a wide range of temperatures depending on the time of year or day. These range from freezing at night during the winter to the high 40s centigrade in high sun during the summer. The high temperatures allied to very low humidity places enormous stress on the body. The three main problems encountered are:
- Heat stroke.
- Heat cramps.
- Heat exhaustion.
- Sunburn.
- Prickly heat.

General factors that affect our ability to withstand prolonged exposure to heat include age, obesity, level of fitness and substances including alcohol, antihistamines and phenothiazines, all of which reduce our ability to get rid of excess heat.

General measures for avoiding heat problems in the desert

- Wear at least one layer of light protective clothing, preferably a natural product like cotton or silk. Avoid shorts and short sleeved shirts.
- Wear a hat in the sun.
- Avoid excessive physical activity. Leave strenuous activities until the cooler evening.
- Relax.
- Stay in the shade off the ground and if possible where there is a cool airflow present.
- Drink frequently and at regular intervals. Do not wait to feel thirsty. In dry, hot conditions the fluid loss from the body is imperceptible.
- Rest frequently if you are performing a strenuous physical task and take more frequent drinks.
- Eat at regular times (food is also a source of fluids).
- Get enough sleep.
- Take at least 5 litres of drinking water per person per day.
- Acclimatise to the heat.

Heat Stroke

A grave condition. The body overheats, and the skin is dry. The sufferer is aware of excessive body heat, and that sweating has ceased. Body temperature can shoot up to 41°C. Headache, fatigue, fast strong pulse, dizziness and vomiting may be warning symptoms - but onset of heat stroke is swift. Unconciousness may follow - and if not treated, convulsions and death. The defining factor is dry skin.

Cause:
Heat Stroke is the result of ceasing to sweat, which in turn is the consequence of using up the salt (sodium chloride) in the bodily system which makes sweating possible. It usually follows heavy exertion under hot conditions.

Treatment:
- Bring down the body temperatures as fast as possible - by wetting clothing, or sprinkling the sufferer, and fanning. Do not immerse sufferer in water.
- Stay in the shade, slightly propped up, preferably in a cool air current.
- Replace fluids with measured intake of salt in liquids (in emergency, intravenously) or in solids.
- When temperature returns to normal, change to dry clothing to avoid chill.

Prevention:
- Maintain salt levels.

Heat Cramps

Abrupt onset of cramps, in legs or arms, or occasionally in the abdominal muscles.

Cause:
As with heat stroke, there is a deficiency of salt in the system.

Treatment and prevention:
- Restore, or maintain, adequate salt intake.

Heat Exhaustion

Symptoms include thirst, fatique, dizziness and disorientation. The skin is clammy, the pulse weak.

Cause:
Dehydration - usually as a result of excessive fluid loss. But in very hot, dry conditions this loss can occur unawares.

Treatment:
- Move to a shaded, cool area.
- Lie down, and drink a little, frequently, with an adequate salt component.

Recovery should be rapid.

Prevention:
- Maintain adequate intake of suitable fluids.

Sunburn

This can occur after as little as ten minutes' exposure. You may not suspect you will suffer at the time - but a few hours later, redness and blistering of the skin will have taken place. Frequent exposure serves to increase the risk of developing skin cancer later in life.

Prevention:
- Wear at least one layer of protective clothing.
- Wear a hat.
- Cover exposed skin with factor 15 sun screen cream at least.

The same applies to babies.

Treatment: treat sunburn as you would treat any other burn.

Prickly heat

This mildly itchy condition can occur when wearing clothing that does not allow for evaporation of perspiration.

Treatment:
- Talcum powder - and adequate ventilation.

Sandstorms

Sand storms can cause respiratory problems, ruin contact lenses, damage eyes and give rise to minor burn-like conditions on exposed skin. The following precautions should be undertaken:
- Cover the mouth, nose and neck with a cloth, preferably moist.
- Breathe through the nose.
- Remove contact lenses: use spectacles instead. (NB: Protective goggles are very useful.)
- Apply chapstick to the lips.
- Stay inside the vehicle.

Food poisoning

Because of both the lack of campsite hygiene and the use of unusual foods from local sources, food poisoning is all too common.

Symptoms:
- Nausea.
- Vomiting.
- Diarrhoea.

Prevention:
- Be scrupulous about your personal hygiene.
- Boil all water unless the source is known to be safe.
- Use canned foods where possible.
- Cook foods well, particularly meat products.
- Wash vegetables with clean water.
- Eat only pasteurised cheese and milk products.

Treatment:
- Give an antiemetic.
- Give fluids only by mouth.
- Give an antidiarrhoeal as required.
- Treat shock if present.

First aid kits

Basic first aid kit:
The following items are recommended to be included in a basic first aid kit and should be carried by each vehicle:
- Gauze swabs, various sizes.
- Crepe support bandages 7 cm.
- Triangular bandage x 3.
- Large pressure bandage x 4.

- Medium pressure bandage x 4.
- Emergency eyewash.
- Large Tensoflex bandage 15 cm x 5 m (x2).
- Adhesive tape rolls 2 cm and 5 cm wide (2 each).
- Medicated swabs (Mediswabs).
- Latex gloves x 3 pairs.
- Scissors.
- Antiseptic solution, Savlon and/or Betadine.
- Plastic forceps x 1.
- Paracetamol 500 mgs x 1 box.
- Cotton wool balls.
- Flamazine cream x 1 tube for burns.
- Jelonet dressings x 1 box.
- Steristrips skin closures (for lacerations not requiring sutures).
- Eyepads x 4.
- Chapsticks.
- Dust masks.
- Glucose powder.
- Salt.
- Antihistamine cream.
- Goggles.

Additional items for a master first aid kit:
- Needles and syringes of various sizes.
- Suturing material.
- Inflatable full leg and full arm splints.
- NaCl 500 mls IV infusion, (sodium chloride).
- Dextrose IV infusion 500mls.
- IV infusion sets.
- Puritabs (water cleansing).
- Plasma expander.
- Imodium capsules (for diarrhoea).
- Metoclopramide or Domperidone for nausea/vomiting.

WHEN ALL ELSE FAILS

When all else fails and you're either lost on your own and/or all the vehicles are broken down or bogged in, then the most essential rule is:

don't panic!

The more experienced desert travellers in the Middle East have yet to find a spot that isn't visited by a pick-up truck at least once per day and lost vehicles are always found. Not so the people who leave them!

Then remember these simple rules:

STAY WITH THE VEHICLE
ATTRACT ATTENTION
KEEP COOL
RATION WATER

Remember: someone will be along eventually, someone knows where you have gone and you've got plenty of water. Don't attempt anything strenuous during the day and erect some form of shade for yourselves. Make the vehicle conspicuous (flags on the antenna, 'HELP' drawn in the sand, the orange marker panels out, a flagpole on top of the nearest large dune or even setting fire to a deflated tyre). But remember, above all else:

STAY WITH THE VEHICLE

APPENDIX I (see page 7)

DESERT TRIP DETAILS PROFORMA		
Date out		
Date Back		
Time Back		
Vehicles types and occupants Leader		
Does the party have a radio	yes/no	
If yes Frequency (MHz)		Callsign:
Does the party have a mobile telephone?	yes/no	If yes Number
Does the party have a radio rescue beacon?	yes/no	
Sketch map of route (continue on an additional sheet and add a marked map if available)		
Deadline for callout of emergency services		

APPENDIX II (see page 7)

Planning Document

Trip to ………….. Dates……………

Outline
- A trip is planned to visit ……………….during the period……………….
- The route will be …………………..……
- The party will consist of …….vehicles
- Everyone will take their own personal and camping equipment.
- Some specialist equipment will be taken by individuals as indicated below.
- Cooking will be undertaken centrally and those responsible for providing meals are listed later.

Participants
- Vehicle 1: …………..
- Vehicle 2: …………..
- Vehicle 3: ……………   etc

Route and Navigation
- Navigator for the trip will be …………..
- Check navigator will be ………….……..
- Sketch maps and route details will be provided by the navigator for each vehicle
- Other navigational equipment (eg GPS) will be carried by:

Responsibilities
- Trip Leader …………….……………
- Recovery Specialist …………….…
- Vehicle Mechanic……………….…
- First Aid…………………………….
- Linguist ……………………….……
- Admin ………………….……….......   etc

Food
- Packed lunch for first day will be provided by individuals.
- All are to provide there own breakfast cereals, snacks and soft drinks
- Each vehicle is to carry ….. 25 litre jerrycans drinking water
- Coffee, tea, sugar and milk will be provided by ……………….
- A substantial evening meal and an easily produced lunch for the

whole party will be provided as shown below:

Day	Lunch	Supper
1	Own arrangement	Vehicle 1
2	Vehicle 1	Vehicle 2

Camping Supplies
The following items are to be provided individually:
- Tents
- Camp beds
- Sleeping bags
- Lights
- Etc.

The following items will be provided by the person listed:
- Cooker: ....
- Portable Shower: ....
- Etc.

Personal Items
Each person should bring their own:
- Clothes, hats, sunglasses, suntan cream
- Washing kit
- Special medical needs
- Torch
- Etc.

First Aid Equipment
Each vehicle should have its own first aid kit. A more comprehensive first aid pack will be provided by ....

Vehicle Spares
Each vehicle will carry the following spares:
- Can of engine oil
- Radiator hoses
- Light bulbs
- Plugs

Other items will be supplied as follows:

Recovery Equipment
Each vehicle will carry
- A shovel
- A short tow rope
- A long tow-rope and shackles

Vehicle .... will carry

- Jacking plates
- Sand ladders
- Winch and snatch blocks
- Air bag

Documentation
Each vehicle and its occupants will need to carry:

Suggested Timings, Route etc.

Day   Route   Distance   Notes